JADE BIRD
SINGING GRIEF

Poems & Art
by Joan Logghe

with
Hope Logghe, Leland Guthrie,
Kaleia Amaya Guthrie, and Corina Sophia Logghe

Wild Rising Press

EVERGREEN, COLORADO

Interior Illustrations: Joan Logghe
Cover Illustration: Kaleia Amaya Guthrie
Editor: Judyth Hill
Book Design: Mary M. Meade
Author Photo: Axle Contemporary

www.wildrisingpress.com
ISBN 978-1-957468-35-8—First Edition

To our family crew and community helpers …

& to Hope and Leland

for facing life and death with so much love and bravery

This family story of birth and death took place on the occupied ancestral homelands of the Tewa people, currently known as La Puebla, New Mexico. The Tewa name of this area translates to "the white divide," referring to the vein of volcanic ash in this area. Our family has called these lands home for the last fifty years. We are grateful for those who have cared for these lands for the millennia before our time here.

Grow some corn—it'll change your life.

…like it has changed everyone who has entered into a

relationship with it.

~Robert Mirabal, *Believe in the Corn:*
Manual for Puebloan Corn Growing

FOREWARD
A Father's Dreams

OUR BABY JADE WAS BORN FULL-TERM WITHOUt a heartbeat on April 1st, 2016. The tragedy took us completely by surprise. She was revived and kept on life support, but when we understood she could never survive on her own, we released her back into the Mystery four days later. Our hearts were broken.

With the help of our families and friends, we pieced together a raft of songs, poems, stories, dreams, and communal rituals to help us navigate the rough waters. Grief and beauty flowed together. We stayed attuned to synchronicities which confirmed our course or offered new orientations.

At the center of our story is Corn, *Zea mays*. The corn chose us, and we chose the corn. The following dreams made this clear.

On January 7th, 2016, several months before Jade's birth, I had a dream. I was barely keeping up with the white-haired Elder ahead of me, who was scaling the steep New Mexican mesa like a mountain goat. At the top edge of the mesa we passed through a rock arch and found ourselves in an ancient Chacoan-style ruin. Remnants of old-growth vigas jutted out from glistening slate-black stone walls. The Elder beckoned me over to the far wall and lifted up a translucent, cream-colored stone door. Behind the door was a nicho, or small hole in the wall, which contained a sculpture made of the same stone. It had the face of a child and the body of an ear of corn. I beheld the beauty and sacredness of the corn-child, and immediately dropped to my knees weeping, praying, and offering cornmeal from the leather pouch at my neck. The strap on the pouch immediately broke and I realized the whole pouch needed to be gifted. As I wept and prayed, a hummingbird flew around the back of my head and began to drink the tears falling down the left side of my face. Awakening from the dream, I heard a voice say, "Your baby is a girl, and her name is Jade." A week later, the ultrasound confirmed she was indeed a girl. It was then my wife agreed that her name must be Jade.

The counterpoint to this dream came several months after burying Jade's ashes in the ground of my wife's childhood home in La Puebla, New Mexico. In this dream, I was standing before a crowd of Corn Elders, whose bodies were upright cobs of creamy yellow-white corn. Their ancient, wrinkled faces emerged from within the pattern of the kernels. Their dense congregation parted, and a taller figure emerged with arms and legs made of red corn cobs. This enigmatic corn person walked slowly in our direction and a woman in front of me fell to her knees and began praying fervently. As the being approached, I felt the power of its presence growing stronger until it became so overwhelming that I woke up.

An hour later I left the house for a morning run, to move the energy through my body and try to make sense of the dream. As I followed the trail through the woods, the dream images came flooding back into my mind and I was again overwhelmed with the potency of the presence of the Corn Elders. Weeping, I sank down onto the wooden bench where I always stopped in the mornings to pray. From somewhere deep in my psyche and beyond, I heard a voice say, "We gave you our daughter, what are you going to do now?" I understood this to be a call to honor the gifts that Jade's life and death had bestowed upon our family and community.

By the time Jade came to us, I had been growing corn in my backyard gardens for many years. My maternal grandfather spent his entire life, after returning from WWII, coaxing corn from the rolling green hills of central Iowa. And he wasn't the first. I belong to a lineage of corn farmers going back five generations.

These corn dreams (along with those of my wife) wove the history and mystery of the corn into the unfolding story of our daughter Jade. Though her time on this earth was brief, her life and death continue to reverberate in the hearts and minds of many. When I plant and tend to my corn each year, I tend to Jade, and the Corn Elders, as well as my own blood Ancestors. In turn, my family and I are pollinated by all the wisdom their combined legacy carries.

Above all, we are grateful to our Amma Joan for capturing the raw essence of that time in the poetry and paintings in this book.

~Leland Guthrie, March 2024

I'M THE MOTHER. I CARRIED OUR LITTLE Jade Bird for nine full months in my womb. I had images of my two little daughters playing together, three years apart they would be, and imagined them running around in dresses picking springtime flowers through Frick Park, right up the hill from where we were renting a home in Squirrel Hill, the place my great Grandmother Sophia lived long ago.

The trees were full of blossoms as we headed to the birth center on April Fools' Day of 2016. Leland and I took our sweet time and savored these moments with just the two of us, listening to music, and I gripped the oh shit handle through each contraction and breathed.

We wandered in to the birth center calm and cool, but then things took that too sharp and too fast life turn that none of us ever expect.

We surprised the bereavement coordinators with our desire to keep our baby with us and bring her home. They labeled us Amish in the medical system, so they had a framework for a family who brings their loved one's body home. We weren't Amish: we were painfully in love with our baby and still needing some more time to say hello so we could begin to say goodbye.

We brought Jade home, swaddled in a blanket, tossing her installed car seat into the trunk so I could hold her in my arms on the way home. I sat next to Kaleia, and we drove home, past the fruit trees that now were covered in shriveled blossoms due to the snowstorm that had hit during our NICU stay.

So much of our story with our daughter Jade Bird was winging it, flying by the seat of our pants, guessing, and saying yes any time we had a question or weren't sure what to do. Yes to offers of help, yes to our gut feelings, yes to ideas for how we might navigate the decisions. Our intuition was strong—we followed the love for our girl, and we said yes whenever anyone asked to help us, because we knew to survive this we needed to say yes.

You took your last breaths
And then all was quiet
We held your body
Heavy and beautiful
Our newborn girl
Fly Free Fly Free Fly Free
Little bird
We sang you a song
To help carry you across
To that place of mystery
Leaving us behind

~HOPE LOGGHE, JUNE 2024

PROLOGUE

I COULDN'T HANDLE IT.

And yet I did, we all did, living beyond the edge of our comfort zone.

Who, I ask you, on our green earth, wants to read about a baby put on life support, just technology away from a stillbirth? Nobody. And yet, those four days were some of the most alive I've felt, living in mystery. A year after Jade's birth and death, I found myself making painting after painting of corn and remembering the harsh times, the ones I didn't want, yet didn't want to forget. The image of her being dressed in a tee shirt I'd decorated with a heart, and her mother— my daughter, Hope—bonding with her, as animals have been seen to bond with their deceased offspring. Jade, lying in state, decked with Gerbera daisies and miniature corn. A devastating beauty. In those holy ecstatic days, we greeted people and explained the corn was from New Mexico. Postpartum Hope standing up, leaking milk, and explaining the corn to the rabbi, the improvised yet grounded ceremony.

Hope and Leland got her out of the hospital in a Moses basket through the back door. They wanted a wake and time with their baby, braving the hospital's common practices. At her cremation, we sang and danced, kept moving our bodies. Is there a word for this post-death state? Beyond grief. Grief to me felt like an invisible machine, an engine that grinds up sadness. You can't rush it— it must move its own gears, the clock of loss. Our family and friends took a vow to run the rapids of loss with us, sing the songs we knew: "One bright morning when this life is over, I'll fly away." We were not okay, but we tapped into a larger-than-life heart space. The shocked parents, grandparents, friends, and family, midwives too, joined us there.

A year later I was still drawing and painting corn. It was relaxing. I was crying from such a deep place, ancestral sorrow. It took a long time and was interwoven with the COVID-19 pandemic, but meds, walking, and friendships helped raise me up. "I once was lost but now I'm found."

When the poet Tess Gallagher lost her husband, the writer, Raymond Carver, she visited his grave daily and people didn't approve when it went on and on. I heard her speak of honoring your own "ecology of grief" even when others disapprove and say, "Get over it already." And here I respect our particular invented ecology, a landscape with love, rain, burial, and corn.

~Joan Logghe, June 2024

CONTENTS

6: Grief

THE SONG I SANG
FOR JADE BIRD

We all come from the Goddess
And to her we shall return
Like a drop of rain
Flowing to the ocean
The mother gives
And the mother takes away
I love the mother

We all come from the mother
And to her we shall return
Like a drop of rain
Flowing to the ocean

Hoof and horn, hoof and horn
All that dies shall be reborn
Corn and grain, corn and grain
All that falls shall rise again

~ATTRIBUTED TO ZSUZSANNA BUDAPEST

1: BLUE CORN/BIRTH

Corn is maiden

Corn is mother

Corn is baby

Corn is sister

Corn is earth

~FROM A SHOW ON NEW MEXICO

PBS, KNME-TV

CORN MATRON

This blue corn is 6–8 inches
in length and I can close my
hand around it. It is cooler
than my body and shines the
color of black pearls. It is the
night sky on silk pajamas,
a dark music, a ceremony
where 100 dark men sit
in rows in the dark.

Blue black and holy
like my father's blue black whiskers.
The union that made me, and mine,
corn girl, the seeds I never planted—
pure potential. It is also joy, just
to stroke the sequential row and
row of living.

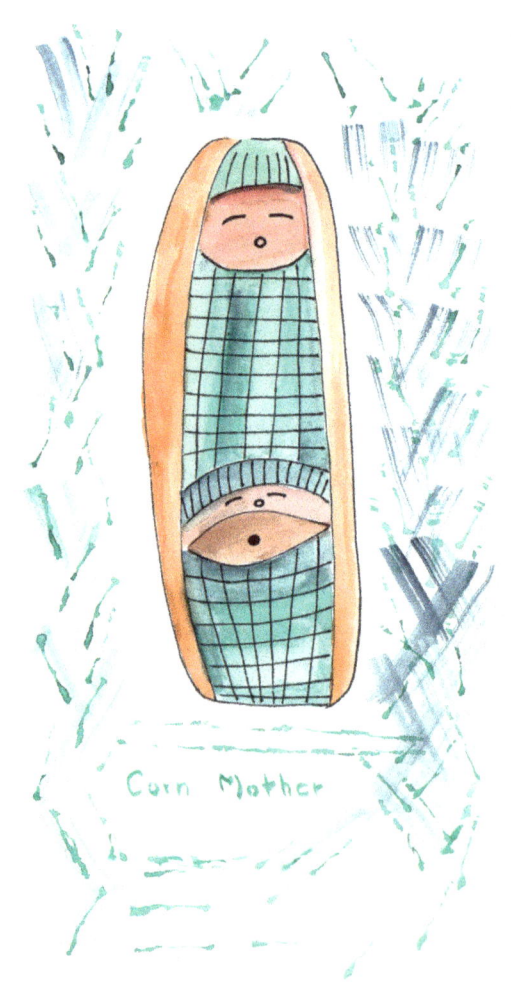

Corn Mother

JADE SEED

Has anyone ever lost
as beautiful a baby
as we have, cheeks
that would have lived
into a thousand pinches,
plump thighs perfectly
lost. It turns out plenty
of people lose daily
though more are born
well. We need loaves and
fishes and water and Miriam's
well, the holy singing
as our baby never got
to and I can't live as if
you never were
and I can't die without
you in me. You bring
hummingbirds to the sweet
and pollinators to buddleia.
Made of white corn and red
as you are, now growing
in loam and your little family
calls you a seed and every
planting is for You.

Hello friends,

We wish we were sending you a healthy birth announcement. Our little baby bird, our little jewel, our seed, Jade Bird Guthrie was born at 7:14 pm on April 1st. 7 pounds 11 ounces.

Sadly, Jade was born without a heartbeat and was immediately rushed to the NICU at the Children's Hospital here in Pittsburgh where she was miraculously resuscitated. But after so long without oxygen, she suffered severe brain damage as well as complications with her major organs. There was never a single moment that she was not in the very best hands. Everyone from the birthing center to the hospital agreed that nothing could have been done any differently.

She's a little butterfly who touched down to land in our hands for just a moment so we could fall so deeply in love. And just as a butterfly only lands for a moment before moving on to the next flower, we are preparing for her flight and ours back to New Mexico.

This afternoon we will be releasing her from all of the machines that are keeping her alive. We ask that you join us in this grief and hold us from afar. Please weep and sing and pray for her in your way. We had a few moments Saturday where her eyes opened, and we locked eyes for a little while. We felt her squeeze our fingers. We felt her present with us as we sang to her. We got to hold her for the first time yesterday. These moments with her are so precious.

We are surrounded by family here and are being very well cared for. We appreciate how you've all been with us so strongly. We love our daughters so much. Our hearts are broken wide open.

Love, Hope & Leland

"A farmer and a midwife do the same work. We learned midwifery from the corn." These are the words of Katsi Cook, a Mohawk elder, healer, midwife, and environmental health researcher who visited last year.

"In the act of growing corn, you begin to feel about corn like babies that are growing," Cook explained. She related the gestational cycle of corn to that of human gestation, and corn's structure to the body of a woman, saying that the corn silks recapitulate our fallopian tubes; the ovaries of the corn are the seed beds where each kernel matures. The "three sisters"—corn, beans, and squash—are symbols of women helping each other and working together, an essential element of the birthing process.

> Hope Logghe, "Birthing back our Roots: Yiya Vi Kagingdi Española Community Doulas" *Greenfire Times: News & Views from the Sustainable Southwest.*

ENCOUNTER

THIS IS YOUR STORY, AND IT HAPPENED.

In the parking lot of Children's Hospital, my daughter Corina said, "Mama, I left my ID at the house. They won't let us in." I knew security here was stricter than an airport. They ask for room number, ID, and code name. Birmingham Doe was the code for our dear baby hovering on life support on this April day, the last one of her four-day life. "Let's see what magic we can work," my eldest said, being close to her sister's pending loss.

I knew the woman sitting on the far right was in charge; I said, "Let's go to her." "Ma'am," Corina said, "I left my driver's license at home"— the woman already shaking her head no and no and absolutely no. "But they are taking our baby off life support," and the woman, not unkindly, said, "I'm sorry." We resolved to have Corina drive back to the house, which was a good hour roundtrip, with all the traffic on Penn Ave and the outer world of roads torn up.

I'd have to go alone up to the fourth floor. I handed the woman my ID for an entry badge that would read GRANDMOTHER under my name. When she printed out the name badge, it did not have my name, but CORINA LOGGHE, AUNT. I held it up for the woman, keeper of the gate, to see—a plea in my eyes.

Looking down and shuffling official papers, she said, "This never happened. You didn't see this." We nodded and thanked her.

On her arm as she handed me my badge, a tattoo of birds flying up in blue ink. *Fly Free*, it said in tattoo cursive. We'd let the baby go that day; Jade Bird was her little beautiful name. We all said we'd get tattoos as if it would help. We straddled worlds that day, singing, "Some bright morning when this life is over, I'll fly away," and I encountered loss like nothing I've ever known and beauty of my two daughters, the mother and the magic one, the revealed beauty of each of them on the April 5th morning in my hometown with its harsh old-world mortality on Penn Avenue in Children's Hospital, a place for other people, certainly not us.

My oldest friend said that losing a baby is not like losing a ten year old or seeing your family all killed + I agree. And someone else thinks I'm not ready to get off anti-depressants. If you come to my house I'll show you a beautiful grave for her ashes. This makes me happy to be sad, the flowers we bought all blooming on the equinox. Yesterday I took a plunge in the pueblo pools. A mikvah I thought, my Jewish New Year. Someone wished me Happy Birthday for it is the earth's birthday, or creation's. People seem to be having opionions + I am susceptible to grief. Don't take my grief away or measure it or think I'm sad. Is sad bad? The world is in trauma + there is only one cure. Hurricane, Earth Quake, Another baby on his way.

corn baby

The baby is a peaceful capsule so pure like a new baby.

Dear Little Big Girl, Remember when ...

I dreamt of holding a girl-child on the banks of a Pittsburgh river sensing something not quite right. We leaned over the waters so you could see your own reflection and your back was made of ashes.

I dreamt of waterfalls and a fat blonde laughing baby boy and an ancient Grandmother walking home, her back to us. Later, as I was driving the road close to home, Hope called to tell me the results of her sonogram and my heart sank knowing she was about to tell me it was you, and you were marking the journey ahead.

Keeper of the bigger secrets, of broken hearts, of hearts rearranging. I never could find you in the realms beyond our everyday, yet there you were all along.

Remember when I drank so many cups of cardamom pu-erh tea with honey and cream that my bones and teeth turned crystalline? We were waiting for you then, and then you came, after sushi songs from Kaleia, little blossoms and all the threads of green. You came and my bones took on the tone of spring and of hearts suspended. I walked up and down the halls of that hospital in the yellow hum of lights and machines. I couldn't find you, but you were there with your chubby hands and the hands of all our beloveds holding us up, from all times and all lands guiding and leading us down those halls. My bones toned, and we all held you one time, and the tone was you, all along. Ringing in new notes, my teeth and bones felt colors never seen and we toned for the mystery, for all the songs, big and little unsung.

Remember when I wondered how you could be so beautiful, so chunky, so perfect—and looking like I did as a baby, a black-haired child from other lands, other people. What a waste, my frugal mind said—how can it be that she is here, grown of my sister's body and all of life and nature conspiring towards this perfect Being and now we have to give her back. To soil and the dust mingled with stars. I don't get it. When I told our friend whose wife had just gone before you, he said he howled for us and you and for his beloved wife traveling home. He came to stand with us and drop his grief-seasoned tears on our family land. And Little Valentino, the Lightning Boy, so wise, he could sing and run and dance! He knew where you went and soon followed you home wrapped in blanket like you. Perhaps you met in that moment where lightning and rainbow intersect.

Remember when those doctors couldn't tell us the truth we already knew. I thought they were dumb, thinking we were dumb, telling us you were very sick. You weren't sick, you were already come and gone. Touching in for a moment here and there. You sacrificed everything to break our hearts open into Love.

Remember when I crocheted that hat of cream cotton that was supposed to be for you? Then I just kept going and I stitched in our hearts and the songs and cries of your parents as I stood sentinel in those yellow halls as your heartbeat went silent offered back into the pulse of the silence. The stitching kept going until the hat was too big and then I unraveled it all.

Remember when I went to Mexico, land of your ancestors, of the corn people. You were everywhere then, hummingbird murals amidst flowers. You were in Chichén Itzá, you built those pyramids, with skulls carved in stone. You were the grandmother selling little bright embroidered dresses, the ones I could not bring home to you. You asked for my tears and bleeding heart to bless the temples and soils where you tread.

Tears led to rainstorms, and we ran for cover, huddled with your people in the jungle green.

And now, Jade Bird, I remember, you were always here and here— everywhere at once. In the sunshine, in the tiny daffodils I planted for you, still emerging every spring. In the first buzz and vibration of the hummingbirds, reminding us it's time to brew sweetness and tend to the tenacious little ones. In all the songs we played and sang for you: "The littlest birds sing the prettiest songs."

In the green stones, blossoms, sprouting seeds, rain and snow and whispers in the breezes, the messages from you— reminding us to ache and celebrate and keep emerging in the spiral of these bones, in these bodies of Love.

AFTER LIFE SUPPORT LIFE

I came here to write about grief, but propriety censored me.
The numbers of griefs are endless; I vow to grieve them all.
Love overtook me, jangling her ankle bells.
The waiter, holding tandoori chicken, said, "All will be well."

The numbers of griefs are endless; I vow to grieve them all.
Across from Children's Hospital I turned to salt.
The man from India House poured water, said, "All will be well."
I came here to write about sky, but there were pebbles in my shoe.

Across from Children's Hospital I found myself turned to salt.
I came here to exorcize ghosts, I found myself rattling bones.
I came here to write about sky, but there were pebbles in my shoe.
I came here with too many books. I came here to write about you.

I came here to write about ghosts—I found myself rattling bones.
I heard a rattlesnake shake. It was my cell phone breathing for you.
I came here with too many books. I came here to read about you.
I have sticktight burrs on my socks. I walk like a penitent Jew.

I heard a rattlesnake shake. It was my cell phone breathing for you.
I found myself drying out tears, my towel wet with the blues.
I have sticktight burrs on my socks. I walk like a penitent Jew.
I wanted to write out the loss. It brought me to holding you.

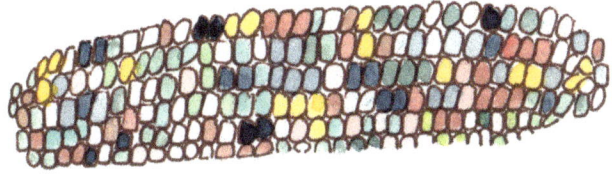

I found myself drying out tears, my towel a deeper blue.
Love overtakes me, her ankle bells jangling.
I wanted to wring out the loss. My eyes focus only on you.
I came here to write about grief.

Our only choice was to follow what felt right to us in such a terribly not right time. We carried Jade's body home in our arms, and it felt right. We laid her in a Moses basket, lined with dry ice, by our bed, and it felt right. We covered her in flowers, with the help of our almost-3-year-old daughter, Kaleia, and it felt right. We sang lullabies to her, invited friends to come fill our house with flowers and say their hellos and goodbyes to our beautiful baby. We received a package with a Pendleton baby blanket and tiny glass gem corn cobs grown by our dear friends in New Mexico, and wrapping Jade in the blanket and covering her in these little jewels felt right. It didn't all have an explanation: we were guessing at a ritual, but knew we needed one. We were sick, with fevers, barely hanging on after so many sleepless nights sitting by Jade's bedside in the NICU, but had to keep it together just enough until we could plant our little seed in the earth.

My mom came out to join us and stayed by our side through the early days in the NICU and through the cremation and through the trip home to New Mexico and at the burial and for the years of grieving we would all do beyond those days. She held me up. When I couldn't cry, she could; when I had nothing left to give, she was there reminding me of how proud she was of me. She wasn't in shock in the same way I was; she was in her own kind of shock. She held me and grieved the tears that I couldn't muster. A mother seeing her daughter lose a daughter is the unimaginable and she wanted to shield me from this pain. And I do believe, through some heroic feat, she did some of the grieving for me, so I didn't have to fall as hard into that abyss.

GLOOMY PANTS

I only want to write about death
and I don't want to write
about death, to be that one,
the gloomy pants, the storm
cloud girl, the eternal pout

I used to be before I got happy,
as I am basically happy
though crying in the bathroom stall
of the Pittsburgh airport.
My hometown is a good place to be sick

If I could measure the magnetism
of how I love this city and family
against how I love my homeplace
and family, this pull-me-hither-
and-yon.

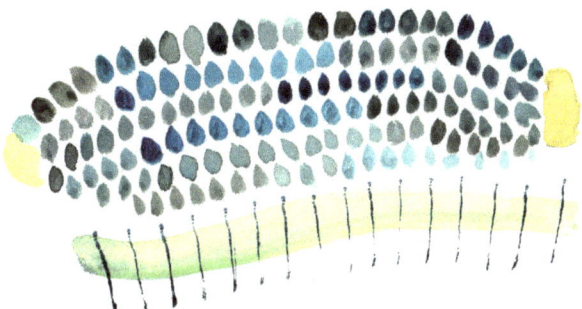

I read a poem on the plane about the NICU.
Last time I read it I'd never been in one.
Little did I know. Little little I did know.

I'd walk the halls, not looking left
or right into another's baby's story,
my own suspended granddaughter
readying to die. Grandpa Charlie sits
by her all night. He holds her hand
A second night. Little little little did I know.

OF COURSE

I can't tell what is more beautiful, the snapdragon
cascading out of the vase or the orchid
blooming a second time.

And I can't tell what is more dangerous, the woman
who cloisters herself in the potted plants
or the floozy swilling another round of mead.

And what is more compelling, the sitcom's canned
laughter or the great books lined up all red
like the soldiers of North Korea on the shelf?

What makes you more anxious, the friend suggesting
meditation or the morning news, which everyone
is busy avoiding or ravenously devouring?

And what is more beautiful, kissing your fat face
the last time or if I never saw you incarnate,
you went right to angel? I'm asking you.

WAKE

That evening people stay awake all night; she is adorned with tiny jewel corn and wrapped in a child's Pendleton blanket, a traditional burial preparation. Many, many Pittsburghers come to pay respects. This is uncommon in Judaism. I read that there is no prescribed ritual for a new babe—so many were lost that they weren't considered alive. Hope tries to explain to the rabbi, and she shakes her rabbinic head. Leland's professor says they will help him with his PhD responsibilities. He tells the story of jumping into the ambulance with no shoes. His mother is arranging the many flowers that fill the house and a nook where Jade Bird lies in state. One of my childhood friends clutches a tight tiny bouquet of red tulips in her hand. She tells me much later that she was uncomfortable. She had no words.

Why do you keep painting Corn?

As if it weren't a universe, as if each kernel isn't carrying a packet from the ancestors, as if there isn't a landscape in each cob we cook + eat.

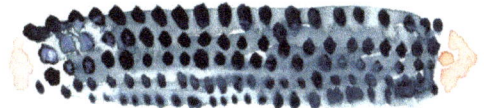

2: FLIGHT

We're losing what we hardly had.

~Leland's mother, Nana April

 *Letter from Hope, Leland, & Kaleia*

Dear friends,

Our daughter, Jade Bird Guthrie, born on April 1st at 7:14 pm, began her journey back into the great ocean of mystery at 12:40 pm on the 5th of April after generously offering us four days of her beautiful, fierce presence. Jade passed away in our arms as Hope and I lay alone together, singing her songs and cradling her, finally free of all of the medical encumbrances that had been keeping her body alive. Her transition was smooth, powerful, and devastating.

We are so thankful to her for those four days she offered us; it was a selfless gift to ease us into our grief and the acceptance of her unique life's purpose. Jade's plan for her short time in this world is being revealed to us moment to moment. The rain of tears that she has inspired with the grief of her tumultuous arrival and untimely departure has moistened unknown crevices in countless parched hearts. Seeds of healing and hope are sprouting amidst the heartbreak. Like a stone dropped into a still pond, the transformative power of Jade Bird's short life is rippling out and embracing our family, our friends, and community in concentric rings of love. People have been able to grieve past losses for the first time; broken relationships between individuals and communities are being mended, and there is pulse and movement where there was once only stagnation.

In a few days we are planning to fly our family back to New Mexico carrying the ashes of Our Little Jewel to be buried in the land of her conception and the land where Hope was born. We will hold a burial ceremony the afternoon of Sunday, April 17th, in La Puebla, NM, and all are welcome. Please let us know if you plan to come and we will send you more information as the details emerge.

As we write this we are surrounded by the fragrance of flowers and our fridge has been filled with food. We feel so cared for by all of you and are so moved, feeling all of your love through this process. Thank you. In Grief and in Gratitude,

Leland, Hope, and Kaleia

CREMATION

They find a green burial mortician. I barely understand but follow our children's lead. She owns a green burial plot and for balance keeps bees and grows gardens with old people. She arranges with the funeral home to allow us into the crematorium to sing and dance for Jade. Hope and Leland push the red button and we sing songs. Later we learn this is called a "witness cremation." The young mortician says the songs are beautiful, she's never heard them before, where did they come from? It's too much to provide a context, so I invent one. I say, Grandpa Charlie taught African and South American studies, so he knows their beautiful yet unfamiliar songs. It is pouring Pittsburgh rain, and the long tables are full of dead drooping flowers, the wilted remains of so much love. The smell of ending. The oven's controls malfunction. Our brokenness and the oven's cannot bear such Beauty. We go back to my niece Lisa's house where the neighbors bring matzoh ball soup, and a lunch meant to celebrate the birth. Lisa lives in Pittsburgh and is a brave soul to help navigate this unfamiliar path and passage.

Corn like music like teeth like pianos like harmonica + harmony like bark more than bite, like bite more than teeth, like a million stalks waving, like fish swimming in fields, like hair made of straw spun into gold, like green dreams, like turtles + turquoise. Small corn

field corn, like opera to radio, like chamber music is to reggae, you hum and you sway. Small corn, deer corn, nibbled by rabbits, harvested by my daughter in memory of her loss. Dear corn, corn maiden you never desert me, you sing in the fields + I only watch.

Loss Corn

WHERE I AM AND HOW MUCH WE LOST

Your story is your story and it happened
To find the great yes
agree to what happened
amor fati—love or fate the rebbe says
you work with what you are given.

I have been given aster blend for mourning
hawthorn berry, Ignatia, mimosa,
rose and agrimony, Grief Relief,
Happy Heart flower essence
and *Natura muriaticum*,
Rescue Remedy and Peyote tea.

I saw my reflection
in the grief lake
of my own face.

Every mirror returned a version of me
I didn't want my family to see.

No wonder we cover the mirrors.

WHERE'S THE BABY?

We traveled back to New Mexico,
Hope's birthplace, where she & Leland met.
Hope in a wheelchair, the old blue
sling variety fetched by the man
in curbside check-in with his wide
Pittsburgh face, part Polish, part
politics, part pleasantry, part football.

And Hope preceded us
after a TSA pat down, her
dear wrecked postpartum body,
her leaky breasts. Her hands holding
on to the little box of ashes.

We followed behind her. Live
Child Kaleia in her father's arms,
and an empty stroller.
At both boardings the flight
attendants took boarding passes
and joked, "Where's the baby?"
Noticing the empty stroller.

"You forgot somebody, no
baby." Corina and I laughed
that sick grief laugh.
"Thanks for reminding us."

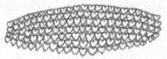

My therapist tried to get me to stop seeing the blessings in everything having to do with how Jade's death unfolded. She called it spiritual bypass. "So much beauty in those four days we got to spend with Jade, and we are blessed we got to bring her home with us." Yeah, yeah, blessings shmessings, in the end you still end up without a baby in your arms. Reminds me of a moment my mom and sister had arriving at the NICU when they got to the parking garage and parked in row F, and my mom said, "We are in row F. F for Fucked." Or another moment when my mom and sister went to Giant Eagle for some snacks for us in the hospital and took photos of themselves pretending to climb up the shelves in an entire aisle lined with matzoh crackers. We needed these moments. They were the balm to soothe and balance the other times, when things were actually fucked. Like screaming at the top of my lungs in our musty basement once Kaleia went to bed, or later, visiting the ER because my heart was so inflamed with grief it hurt. I would dance and contort my body to somehow move the grief out of my chest because it just was too much to hold.

3: BURIAL

Every time I see a baby

Every time I see

a baby

Every time

I see a baby

your face.

BURIAL

The preparations made, a scavenger hunt
for death, for beauty. Flowers and jade beads,
and a golden rain tree chosen by Tia Corina—
100 guests held her.
Kissed the blanket with the ashes snuggled inside.

Big sister Kaleia was three, in her tutu phase,
wearing one in the airport and plane,
and at the burial ceremony. After the ashes
were passed around wrapped in a Pendleton
blanket, Hope and Leland knelt over the grave
and Kaleia behind them put a rose in her dad's back pocket
then a hand on each of her parent's backs,
winged child. I dare you to forget this.

Afterwards some people said this was not
their cup of tea. Others said they felt it among
the most meaningful things in their life.
A naked baby doll appeared
on the mound. A gift, sister to sister.

We filed by, placing jade beads
and flowers, planting the golden rain tree

which has four seasons,
leaf, flower, lantern, seed.
Even now it grows.

HUMMINGBIRD

Your story is your story and it happened

Sad is sad. Grief is grief.
I found a dead hummingbird
in the rainwater after we placed
your little pot of ashes
in the ground. Little hummingbird.

Wrapped in felt made by your father
tied with a woven inkle belt,
sung to with songs from Africa, Peru,
Kaddish from the Jews,
purified with sage and copal.

Brief is brief, 4 days of perfect love
(no presence, no ego, what is consciousness?)
in a beautiful present, wrapped and delivered
back to the mother. Your Tia Corina singing you
every bird song sweetly in Spanish and English.

A secret life lived in the family, as if, as if
the life support sound. The nurses felt it.
There was a being, a child
with a perfect body, except never a breath,
not a cry. From love back into Love.

BROKEN VESSELS

At the end of the burial
she broke a pot into the grave
beautiful, beautiful, just as you
were too perfect to stay

At the end of their wedding
they broke a pot, beautiful
too beautiful, to invite even
the broken into their deep days

after all the crying was done
the broken accepted
the invitation

EVERYWHERE JADE

Jade is everywhere. On the flap of a book
about the Chelsea hotel, in Rudolfo Anaya's
children's book *The First Tortilla,* in two
little turtles, one dead and one living
in the jade Buddha my mother once wore
in the eight jade plants in our greenhouse
in my jaded heart since she died, in ashes
ashes all fall down and in the burial site
I call plot or grave or Jade's garden
and the children, the children dancing
around the airport at Midway, the story
I tell again and again, they are wearing
pink and purple, they are dancing
and the little one always seems about to fall
never does and she is the Jade we won't have
and today again, in the thrall of antidepressants
and the agony of lost election for a woman just
my age, the tears are full of jade so they must
be green tears, turtle tears, pipelines of oil
the dark sludge of it, and protests, and head
scarves on righteous women in our town
and Jade is everywhere, and my friend says
You write about her. I will be twice as political.
I absolve you. I have swum in these jade green seas.

RAINWATER

After we mourned, after we buried the ashes
of Jade Bird, we tossed in flowers and jade beads
my children leaned over the grave of my grandchild.
After we fed 100 people, after one said,
This is not my cup of tea, after others said,
This was one of the most meaningful things,
after we had completed some of the grief work,
Tauz brought us a quart jar of rain. She said,
After the mourning on our pueblo, we wash
in rainwater.

This was Hope's last day at home.
Time to catch a plane. We poured rainwater
on our hands, maybe on each other's hands
I don't remember. We sang a little, spoke
of the blessings and teachings from Jade Bird,
a child that lived four days on life support in my home
city of Pittsburgh. We'd all been through so much,
my daughter, son-in-law and three-year-old Kaleia.
We stood on this sunny hillside, next to the lightning-struck
cottonwood tree, the Shaman tree, not a cloud in sight,
the clear blue of sky. There is no way but to say this,
a column of rain, a cylinder, a shaft of rain fell only on us,
the mourners, the sacred ones, twice blessed. We felt joy.
A hummingbird zoomed by us. We were all buzzing and blessed.

Then Hope and her living child got into the car and drove away.
Time for that cup of tea.

I kept waiting for the old
Jewish lady to show up and help.
I realized I was already there.

Oseh shalom bimromav,
Hu yaaseh shalom aleinu,
vál kol Yisrael. Vimru: Amen

Let the Great Name be blessed forever and ever.
Let the Name of the Source of Life
be glorified, exalted, honored.
Though the One is beyond all the praises,
blessings and adorations we can utter.
And let us say Amen.

~Excerpt from Mourner's Kaddish

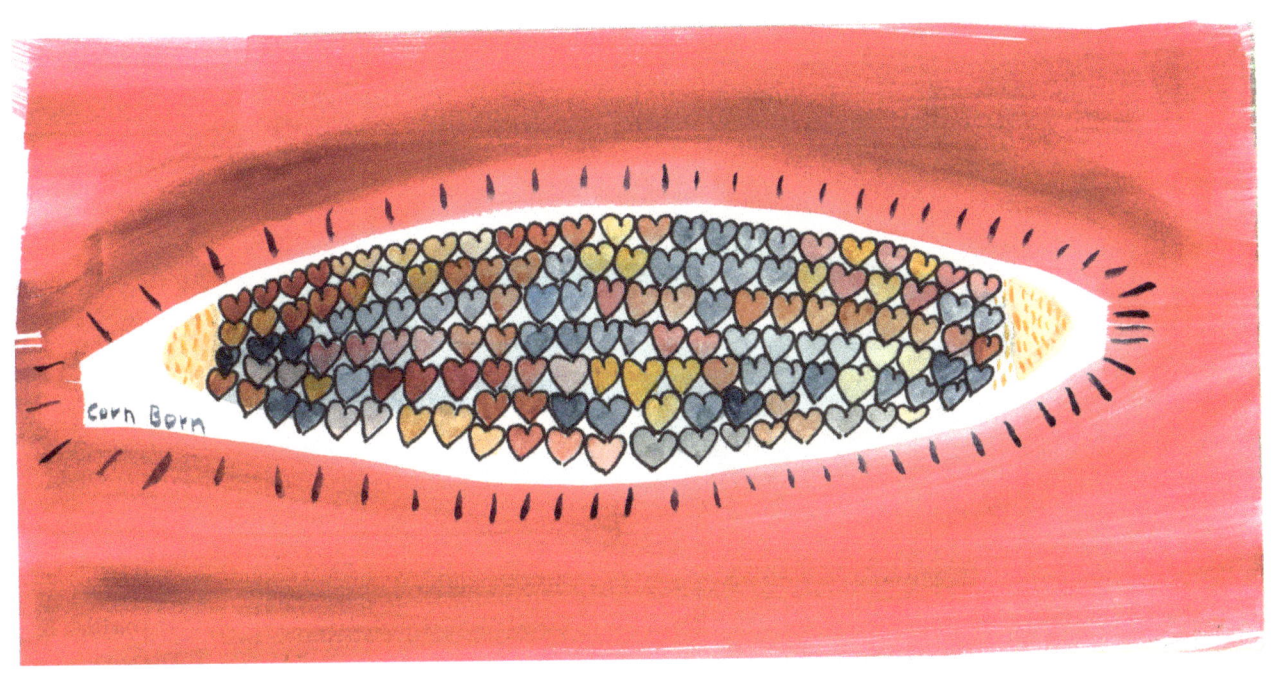

4 : PLANTING

Long is long

Short is short

Each life is complete

~Zen Saying via Alvaro Cardona-Hine

Alvaro wanted very much to make us a Zen garden but was too weak.
We accepted his offer, saying yes, despite the impossibility.

THREE MONTHS

She wears a jade
hummingbird necklace
I wear a jade chick

Life irritates
the pearl in me
thankful even so

Little Jade
today you visit
in the form of sobs

I wrote about feeling as if I were wearing an old-fashioned
black veil, with little specks or sequins on them, so dark is my mood.
Then, as if on assignment, a veil drops over my left eye
and a week later my right. Floaters, which everyone has had.
But just as I get grumpy that folks don't appreciate this level
of grief, so my somatic veil is worse than they know. I have trouble
    driving,
reading on the computer and seeing this beautiful landscape. The veil
    lasts
6–7 weeks, and after my trip to Pittsburgh is gone. It may come back.
The eye doctor actually walks over and hugs me. I told her I had been
    crying

a lot, in grief. She did not ask the source and I didn't volunteer it. I
asked again,

"Can crying hard cause this?" She shook her head, didn't affirm or
deny.

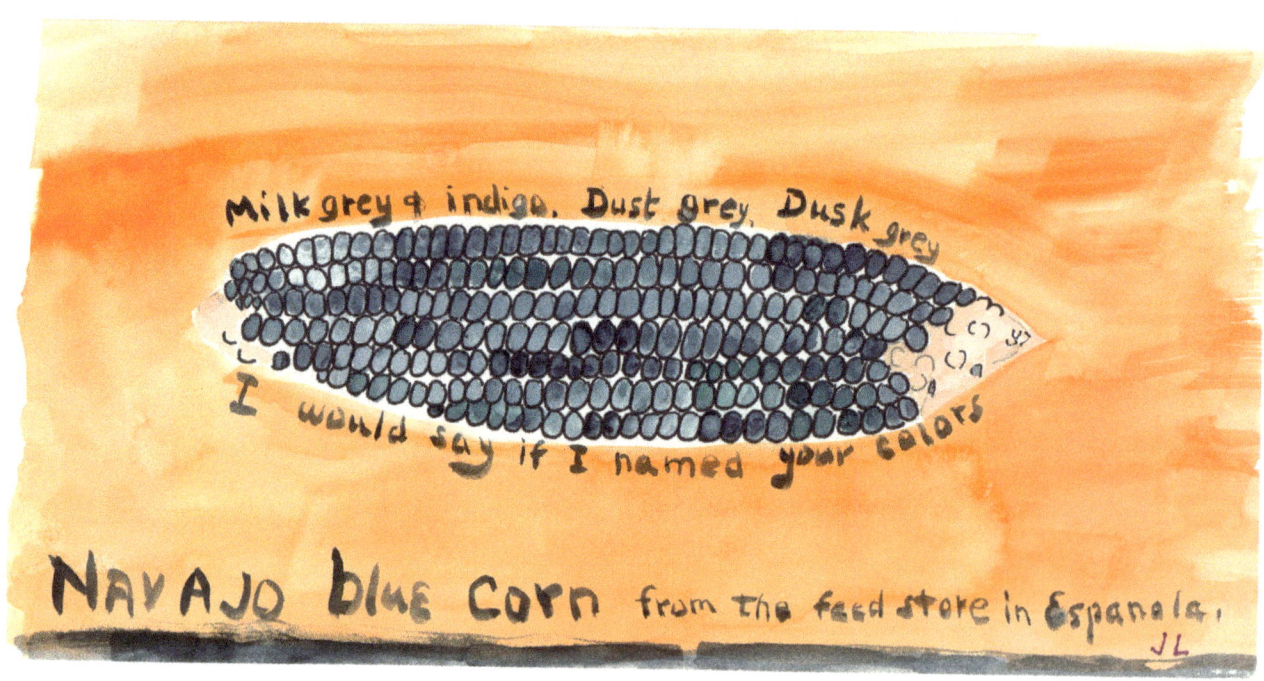

Milk grey & indigo. Dust grey, Dusk grey
I would say if I named your colors

NAVAJO blue Corn from the feed store in Espanola.

JL

LITTLE TWO DAUGHTERS

Your story is your story and it happened

The desert teaches me not to be alone
except all the time, to sit
in a circle and laugh
that stars still exist
have existed always
the light we cannot see by day
the faint torch of night

Last night I thought of her
little daughter who walks
in the dark and how she
had a baby that flew away early
the word miscarriage is not
what she said. She walked
in the dark every night
it became almost a bone
of contention as I lit my light.

I love her, daughter I saw only once again
at the burial of my own girl's child.

The stars are there even
in the daylight and we are made
of their dust. That's what everybody

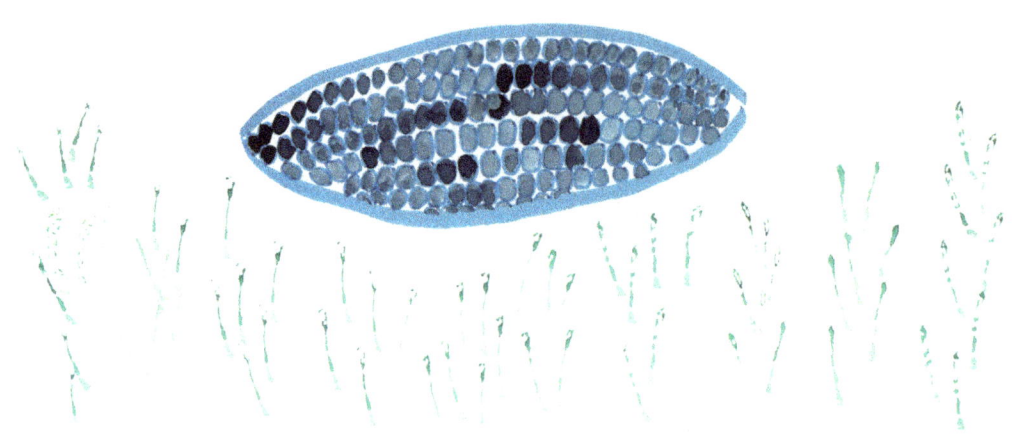

in the know says though I can't
imagine. I moved to the desert
so I could learn myself away
from city. I live here so my sky
carries up random prayers.
Little two daughters who walk
in the dark. There are countless stars.

THE WEEPERS

Give me the weepers
I cannot abide by anyone
who smiles. A smiling woman
offers to speak with me. I run.
I'm failing grief's sobriety test.
Grandmother, I can't write a straight line.
Bird for Beti and Birdie, great

and perfect, as she was so chubby
and fulsome, her name too beautiful
from a list Hope obsessed over,
I wear a jade bird necklace.

My mother said *Grandbabies,*
she called them her dividends
banking on their through line
in Pittsburgh. This begins
with my birth in Pittsburgh,
didn't end

with my grandgirl's death.
Grief comes in circles.
I want to tell the story straight
but the story bends.

The blue black corn my husband grew, planted last year + harvested by birds + a childhood friend. The blue black lustrous as satin, dull + shining in each kernel, far from the vivid luminescence, almost translucence of freshly picked. Gone, given way to a patina of milk gray + indigo, dusk gray, dust gray I would say if I named the colors. + the grandfather kernels to plant alive forever. It draws me into death at mass handing me and keep the boy Blue Soldiers of North Korea marching in threatening synchronized step. Rows + order of the cob, a village an audience at La Boheme reaching for their black handkerchiefs in the dark. Why is the word corny critical, when this community of seed is the holy carried forward, a single life lived variously, a multitude of yes + no, a capsule of blue, blue, this Navajo corn seed from the food store in Espanola. The precision of baby teeth biting into life You, corn, had a secret swaddled under your husks, that only on picking and unwrapping, undressing you, is sacredly revealed.

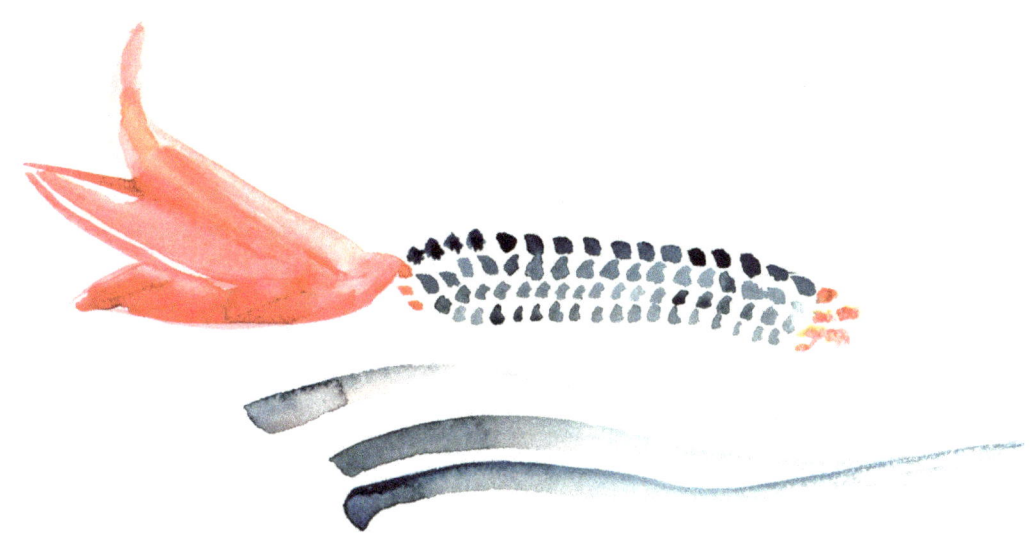

5 : UNVEILING

Love is one side of the coin,

Grief is the other.

~Neighbor, Scott Bennett

~

We are the rememberers,

and soon we will be the remembered.

~Neighbor, Julie Bennett

CORN CEREMONY

My daughter Hope sent out a photo of a rainbow over our house. This is not an uncommon sight, as we live where the rain meets the sunlight, but this photo by our dear Carol Nieukirk came at a time out of summer season but still in grief season. It is the first *Yahrzeit* of our baby Jade Bird's life and death on April 5. I posted this on Facebook, always with my doubts about bumming people out in this already fraught world. But when I heard back from 83 people, with many amazing comments, my second-guessing calmed down. You should see how quiet I have been.

My old friend Ellen Schmidt spoke about playing on all 88 keys—we don't just tinkle along merrily in the right hand of it, but submerge in the left-handed bass, all the octaves of emotion. I think of the most famous koan of one hand clapping. I think of the right hand not knowing what the left hand is doing. Maybe if we embrace the darkness and light, we don't get into the politics of denial and separation, we'd have a better chance.

I also recommend to myself to be kind and openhearted to I and Thou, to not second-guess so much and just move. I have all along been saying I am doing nothing—I am not writing. But I have been entering scraps of writing about Jade, and my own reaction to her absolute purity and our infinite loss. When I printed them up, with no thought of good or bad, there were pages and pages. The miracle of my own perception of nothing being indeed something. Jade was a being of intense beauty and a gift beyond our understanding.

I call her almost a female savior. My husband says she came to break open our hearts and reiterates all the blessings she brought. He has not been the same, and in a good way. Sita Jameson, singer of kirtan and sacred chant, said that Jade did more in her brief life than many

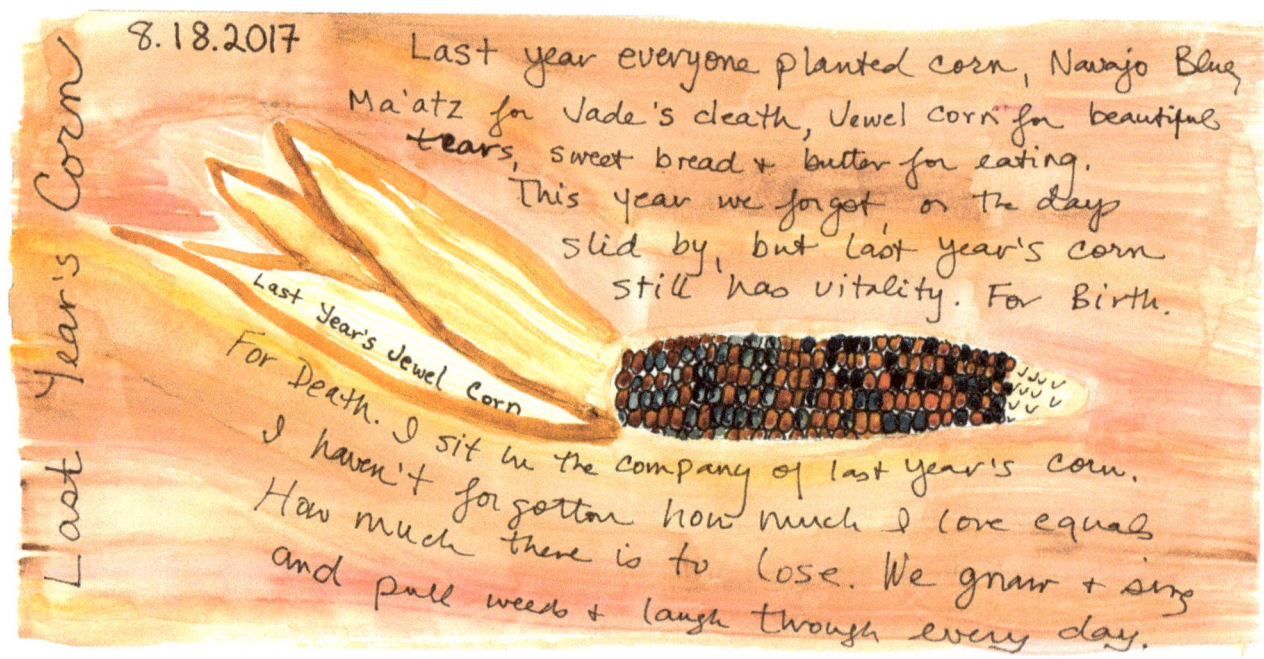

Last Year's Corn

8.18.2017 Last year everyone planted corn, Navajo Blue Ma'atz for Jade's death, Jewel corn for beautiful tears, sweet bread + butter for eating. This year we forgot or the days slid by, but last year's corn still has vitality. For Birth.

Last Year's Jewel Corn

For Death. I sit in the company of last year's corn. I haven't forgotten how much I love equals How much there is to lose. We gnaw + sing and pull weeds + laugh through every day.

people ever do. At nine months, Hope and Leland came back here to New Mexico, their fourth visit from their Pittsburgh home to their heart home. Their friend would lead a ceremony. People in their community had planted corn in the spring in honor of Jade, a special white corn used in Mayan ceremonies of birth and death. To even see the corn they harvested was a miracle. Noble, large white ears of corn, scraggly little crooked ones four inches long. Hope, my daughter and mother of two daughters now, one on earth and one in the spirit world, said the sight of the corn is something she never expected. It was a great beauty. And that hollow deep grief machine again.

Our right hands did know what the left hands were doing. It was many hands for two days, shucking, roasting, grinding, preparing. This little spirit was so honored in her brevity, so present and so alive in us. At one time I stood full of gratitude for her and knew I would not be the same without her coming and going. Still, I sobbed deeply when her story was told. The left and right hand together make corn grow and fire catch, and prayers fly. I have felt almost mute, but today was moved to write, thanks to the Facebook "likes" and responses of friends on this crazy internet world in this crazy life and time. Men and women too, both hands. Yes and No, the duality and just us sitting around today with plum tree in bloom, and the flowers we planted a year ago for Jade's burial, blooming again.

Traditionally everyone would fly in for an unveiling, within the year after a death, to see the headstone and say Kaddish. The cousins, the aunts, they all traditionally gathered to weep a little more, place a stone on the grave, and then eat.

We have a beautiful headstone, and the poems I wrote will be my unveiling for my daughter and family. There was a time last summer when I felt as if I had a virtual veil. I wanted a warning sign that it was not business as usual. I wanted people to stop asking, "Are you writing?" Then I had an interior or somatic veil and could not see well. I am grateful that gradually, during my own trip to Pittsburgh, my eyes cleared. So now I see, gratefully, in stereo. I write to all of you, unveiled.

Jade Bird Guthrie

April 1, 2016 – April 5, 2016

Fly Free Little Bird

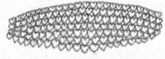

We looked for tangible objects that brought us meaning. One was holding these little corn cobs in our hand. They felt like the little jewels that Jade was. Leland and I had grown corn for our 10 years together; we had many dreams of corn, and these little cobs were like little reminders of our treasure. Once she was cremated, many cobs went with her, and a few stayed with us on our altar, to hold and remember that fleeting physical time with our baby. I bought a little turquoise pendant and wore it; it had a corn maiden with a baby on one side, and on the other, a corn maiden. As I flipped it back and forth, it felt like my experience, of being with baby, then without, all so quickly.

ABSENCE OF OBJECTS

Everything reminds me of you, the turtle
for mother earth, the acorn from my city,
wine cork for your months in Santiago, Chile,
the jacks for how we never played them,
daughter of an older mother.

The butterfly you said landed on your hand
and left, your hand above your brief baby's
perfect body. The jawbone from the elk
your husband shot. The buckeye for my childhood.
The clay mother holding a clay baby, as your
child was clay. The cat's-eye marble, the fish.

The daylight, the lunch time, the afternoon.
When I say, "Good morning," I mean can you tell
I'm swimming in the past? When I kiss
you does it translate as, "Everyone
must die, some sooner, some late?"
The tiny monkey in the red cap, the corn,
the corn, the corn, the bone button
is made of Her, the holy dirt, the pumpkin seed,
the singular, the plural, all things rhymed
and cacophonous, are leading me to Her.
The pot shard from Pojoaque, in the first
shovel of New Mexican dirt. The poker chip,

the arrowhead, the domino, the die. The whole
universe of objects and the negative
space absent of Her. Just the other
day, and this one. The scissors.

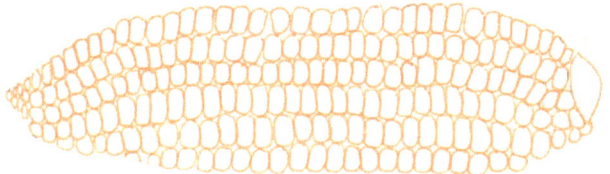

BIRTHDAY

For my daughter Hope

You don't know how to celebrate the birthday
of the child who came and went. You said
last year she was a butterfly that touched down,
holding your hand above her life-supported body.

You are fielding phone calls, opening chocolate
and accepting a meal of jade corn. You lament
not having the moment to bond as she was whisked
away and away she stayed. Nobody could be

as brave as the two of you. At least nobody I know.
You attend the Children's Hospital's lunch for grieving parents.
You walked Jade Bird out of that same place
for a wake, becoming Amish and dignified.

I look up the Jewish mourning rituals, knowing I am
not living under that heavy-duty lawyer God.
Back then they verily erased a baby
if it lived less than thirty days. Back then, in shtetl

or in Kiev, many were lost. Move on move on move
on beyond cold kitchen and pogrom.
I dream of a gigantic key and a massive rose.
Things feel heavy to turn, too fragrant and thorny.

You look up animals to see if they bond with stillbirth
and they do. A porpoise can carry around her baby for weeks.
You read me a poem, we talk on screen, scanning each
other's distant faces, made close by silicon and current.

I invite the Jews to gather by the grave, cut flowers,
unveil the small stone with her name and dates.
Chant the ancient syllables of Mourner's Kaddish.
The candle burns all night despite the wind.

JADE BIRD

No one will ever have a name as beautiful
as Jade Bird. I stand at the garden we try
and try to plant over your memory.

The rabbits eat the jade-green leaves
from the Hen and Chicks, every optimism
perishes as you did. How can anything

shore us up for these losses. You so beauty,
you at the end of the day. You touch and go.
You hummingbird girl, you unlived more

than many lived life. Your absence. I stand
and read the stone. Thunder rumbles
in Santa Fe on the eve of the Folk Art Market.

Humans come from Cuba and Mozambique.
From Pakistan and Mexico. I could name
every place you're not and will never go.

My friends turn seventy and brag about their travels.
I hide under a rock. The only thing that soothes
is swimming back and forth in the outdoor pool.

My grandson firing fireworks in the parking lot
by the barn. The chickens roosting. The Rufous
hummingbirds clicking and fighting. The mosquitoes

arrive with stripes on their knees.
Not even with a gin and tonic under my belt.
Can I handle this grandmother's grief.

MATRILINEAL

If my mother had been here
she would have worn grief's mask
and met me at the airport
in raw mortal Pittsburgh.

She would have said, move on.
Look ahead. You can lick anything
even this sad Lithuanian loss. Be more
Hungarian, it was Fate, *beshert*, meant to be.

But I am not my mother, not anything,
no way, no how, like her.
While she shines, I darken. I hark
to an earlier time before we met.

It seems odd that she bore me
with this gift for darkness. And
I bore her, with her klieg light love.
Oh Jade, you are our lineage.

No pogrom for you, no war,
no starvation, no fear, no tears,
the absolute peaceful one. Great
in beauty at the end of the line.

WILD EDGE OF SORROW

I am sure now
my home is in the world
not so tied to one
place I've lived in
all my life

What wild grief
told my sorrow
it could hold me
around the throat
like a rough sort of love

I can't write about
that little baby
who was my next love
and broke my heart
into a thousand birds

You can't give grief
a deadline, why people surf
or climb rock face
makes sense tonight
we are so small and on edge

6: GRIEF

Kaleia dictated these little "prayers" to Hope:

On the other side of the mountain
on the side we can't see,
where mothers, fathers, sisters, brothers
gather someday
on the other side of the mountain.

Who is great
I love you
Jade you're my sister
Jade bring back her heart
Bring this rock to your heart
(as she held the rose quartz to her heart)
We can visit you every time.

~Kaleia Amaya Guthrie

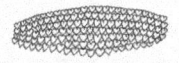

Unwrapping each cob
Of jewel corn
Eager to see your face in each one
Their silks dark like your silky black hair
Each cob like unwrapping a gift
Excitement coursed through our bodies
As we finally get to see all the colors of your precious jewels
As we finally get to meet your children
That cob that I cradled by my heart like I had cradled you for too short a time
That cob that I cried to let go of as we pulled seeds and nestled them in the earth
Just like we had so recently laid your beautiful bones deep down into that soil
To see who might grow
That cob that was near your body those few days felt like it still carried your essence
Now I'm surrounded by babies from those kernels
And it feels like you are filling our home back up now
With the sustenance that was you and was your life
Jade Bird, my sweet
You live on in such beauty now

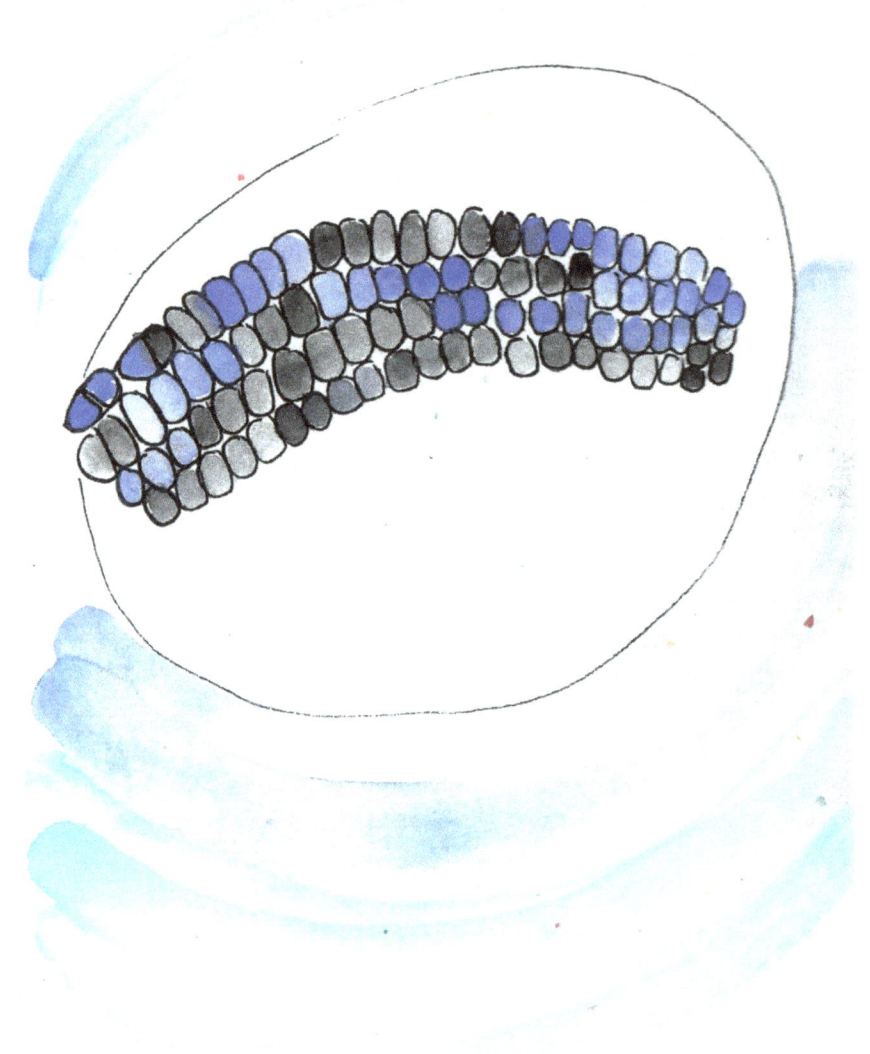

BLUE CORN AND RED-WINGED

for Darry and Tricia

Halfway through the book I'm writing about grief,
the blue corn began chirping, sounding like pebbles
over pebbles, and my daughter said, "Mama," she likes
to call me that even now, "The birds are devouring the corn."
I would have preferred if she'd said "devastating"
of said corn since that is the word of the grief hour.

As it happened, a grade-school friend
and his wife were here and offered to help, as you
were napping when the red-winged blackbirds struck.

Hence the three of us and my daughter sallied forth
into the blue corn and harvested the pathetic,
bird-pecked and blighted ears, only three or four inches.
We must have forgotten to dance for them at planting
or didn't sing the blue-corn chant, diminutive as they were.

Even so they glowed with a fresh blue translucence
enough to put us into corn-harvest trance.
We picked them all in a hot September hour, so far from
a New York minute, heat mixing up blue corn with childhood friend,
who had nothing to do with blue corn,
but it's hard to separate today from childhood.

We shucked the corn, I roasted and ground and made *atole,*
a blue gruel served up with devastating raspberries, maple syrup,
half & half, and for a nourishing moment we were full and happy.
It's as if we'll never know grief again.

GERBERA DAISY

When you died, little impossible one, you met me
at the impasse, the hover point between life
and life-support machine winking red and green
lights, so beautiful in the photo I took and lost,
the mechanical breath that was all you had to give.
Won't it be hard to have your grave site
right west of the house, an old friend asks?
Nothing now that isn't hard, I get to visit you, choose
when I want to sample the miracle. I stood at the corn
and realized my life would be emptier without you.

Gerbera daisy is your flower. The one goldfinch among the house
finches, the woodpecker. All beauty whispers your absence.
Your father sobs at the grave, calls you by your nickname
Jade, Bird di, di, who never heard a name.
I wear a jade bird on my throat. I dust the jade
Buddha on the mantel. This one your mother brought from
Thailand as a teen. Now I handle this blessing, handed by heavy-
handed life?

I DOTE

I dote on grief
I dote on emptiness
My little big girl sings
Jade di di di, she died.

I dote on absences, rules
that break. A tape measure
showing how she was stretched
out. I dote on memory lost

the loss hurts too, memory
of intense once upon
a blessing way that may or may
not have worked. Maybe she

was indeed blessed. I dote.
A grandmother after all
like Hilary, our presidential candidate,
only less present and more
prescient, and neither of you win.

MANTEL

It called me and then I called you
and the way you tell it, the doctor
has his own story, bag of sticks,
sitting by fire. You are called by copal,
called by blue corn or jewel corn or
maatz' corn labeled Jade's life & death
corn on my mantel. I dust the pollen
from the ledge. My house is full of shrines
to the living and to the dead. The dog Ziggy
next to my widowed mother next to
grandchildren next to a string of birds
from India weighted by a bell.
The heart-shaped stones gather over
your ashes. Every day I water the golden
rain tree. Every day I filled the feeder
for hummingbirds, what comfort
in the word sweet. The sweet world
goes on without you and yet you are
the strongest presence, tiny ghost,
illuminated one. It was as if a small
female savior appeared. "She died
to break us, to crack us open," my husband
says. He calls her Jade Bird which I can't
her name is too beautiful to say. I call

her only Jade. Her photo on the mantel
the pollen gone, the flower fades
and is replaced, waters freshened.
We cut the stems to draw fresh life.
There is a tiny license plate. The kind
you see at airports and tourist shops.
JADE, a New Mexico plate in turquoise
and gold. My daughter bought all
the store on the Plaza had, gave me one
though I'm not sure I want it, a tiny token
keepsake, memento, metallic love,
the license for you to fly away

FLY FREE LITTLE BIRD

We're living *La Bohème* without the soprano
the word of the year is "devastated"

And what is more beautiful, kissing your fat feet
the last time or if I never saw you incarnate,

you went right to angel? I'm asking you.
They come to me as chorus and as solo

the tiny heroine has left the stage
I am/you are/she is/ a conjugation

we stand by a grave one January night
a siren in the black background

Candle shuts off, the white dog
sighs a little his Samoyed sounds

A goodnight wrapped in a goodbye befriends us
as we lay this sweet one down.

from Hope's Pages

We wrapped you in white silk
Held you as you were exhaled across the veil
And my milk dripped onto your forehead
One last attempt at feeding you
And you, my beloved,
your breaths have stopped
So quiet and peaceful
But my tears pour
As my breasts empty to you
My mother body tries to feed and warm you
I'll do it in my dreams now

TWENTY-SEVEN SORROWS

with thanks to Michael Ondaatje, via Miriam Sagan

Like a Tuvan throat singer
like licorice that turns your mouth black
like a popsicle of dirt
like a love song written by a vulture
like a child articulating a soliloquy
like tremendous relief before the applause
like the devastated spoken in German
like a storm cloud singing opera
like a terrible two, an awful nine
like the sevens in multiplication
like a sponge wrung out by a therapist
like an irritation that doesn't produce a pearl
like your father swallowing his last oyster
like the word "Oy!" a Yiddish punishment in vowels
like a shattered cell phone
like knees everywhere from too much prayer or gardening
like the impresario producing the funeral
that will sell out
like enough is enough
like just try and get over it already will you
like dynamiting the storyline
like 10,000 worries weren't enough

like rattling our human cages
like God heard me say we have been blessed
no matter what,
like the Evil Eye wasn't a made-up thing
like the meaning fell out of the story
like buying a meter that measures darkness

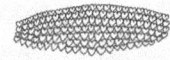

Hope's Dream:

In my dream I was in a gallery, and I saw a door.

It said "Corn" and I walked up to the door and opened it and went in.

In this room, the walls were lined with shelves crowded with corn maidens.

I was looking at all the beautiful corn maidens and then, on the other side,

this piece caught my eye.

It was a carved canoe of mother-of-pearl, opalescent white,

filled with four different grandmothers, holding babies.

Two were holding little babies and two were holding corn babies.

There were two hummingbirds carved into this canoe.

The grandmothers had their mouths open like o's and they were singing lullabies.

LEFTOVER GRIEF

with thanks to André Breton

My grief with its hair hung down
its back and its *La Llorona* voice
with its clothes torn by screams
and its manic feet, with its feat
of shoehorns and its beak of time.
My grief with my brother driving
a siren truck, with my brother
at a wheel and it spins roulette.
There are numbers and colors and
they all land on death. My grief
with my mother's handkerchiefs
with the blue initial cheering me
to tear, with a long gone nasal drone
and apostrophe. My grief with a perfume
called Magritte, with cosmetics made
of forest-fire-burnt logs, lipstick made of coal.
With the kohl-rimmed eyes and a brimming
brew of tea. With a tea steeped out of afterlife
and rue. With a missed chance or regret at what you said.
My grief with a bottle of blue wine
from the bluest flower. With a wine brewed
of oak leaves and acorn flour.
With a wine decanted and you get the dregs.

My grief with a descant as you descend to hell.
Where pomegranate seeds ruin everything.
Where looking back makes love into salt.
Where the salt turns black, dissolves into saline soil.
Where the soil is arid now a hundred days.
Where the drought has planted dust and tumbleweed.
My grief is the burn which masquerades as sun,
the body weather that belies the fact.
My grief with a headstone trying to turn its back.
The arrogance of death and its cold stare.
My descendants facing forward even so.
My grief with an able-bodied child toddling away.
With relief a good ways down the road.
The rabbi says the tunnel at the end
of the light. Who said, "This too shall pass"
meant what will stay?

GRATITUDES

To Hope Logghe, Leland Guthrie, and Corina Logghe for creating ceremony and meaning in the midst of sadness and for encouraging me to pursue this project. To big sister Kaleia Amaya, for growing so strong in the wake of loss. To rainbow sister Krystal Pearl, who helped plant flowers in Jade's garden.

To my Michael, who stayed home and kept it together. To our dear friend Thayer Carter, whose woodcut, Peruvian Black Corn, ignited my obsession.

To Leland's family, who gathered to love and honor Jade Bird. To my niece Lisa Slesinger, who accompanied us with such bravery. And to the rest of the Logghe, Slesinger, Guthrie, and Faidley crew. To Grandpa Charlie, Erin Guthrie, and Cassie Smith, who embodied deep love, and April Faidley, who arranged flowers and drove all night from Indianapolis. To Leland's family friend, Lisa McIlvried, who researched funeral alternatives.

To Tauz Tamupovi and Molly Ruiz, who sent the original baby Glass Gem corn and Pendleton blanket to us in Pittsburgh. To the midwives and the Mid-Atlantic Mothers' Milk Bank, who embraced our family. To my friend Nancy Tapper Smith, our extra grandma, who sent the amazing egg rolls on our last night in Pittsburgh. To the green funeral director, Kristin Hauman of The Natural Funeral Company, and death photographer, Jenny Stein, who captured the beauty in the tragedy.

To Mark, Tara, and Nila for being housemates and extended family. To Lila Dow for her bounty of white corn. To Joshua and Kirsten for the photos, tents, and tables. Sol and Kendall for setting up a GoFundMe account for Jade's ceremony and burial.

To everyone who contributed to that GoFundMe account and Michael's sister, Sharon, who gave us airline miles for our family's travel back to New Mexico.

To my dear brother Carl and my sister Carol Slesinger for never-ending support and the van to the airport. To Julie and Scott for holding us as family then and still now. To Tricia Vigilante and Robin Rodar for their healing friendships.

To my assistant and poetry doula, Sal Maxwell, who helped me organize, which is no small gift, and saw the book in its beauty before I did. I could not, absolutely not, have done this without her.

To Wild Rising Press—editor Judyth Hill whose ear for poetry encouraged my better poetic self to be heard; she took what I said and made it what I meant. And huge gratitude to designer Mary Meade, who had such sweet patience with this complex mix of image and text. As Judyth said, "She thinks in image."

To Hope's friends and colleagues from Tewa Women United for honoring the life of Jade Bird at her burial.

Our overflowing gratitude to Mark Jensen, Wolf Martinez and Michael Oullette, Zev Friedman, Carol Nieukirk, Scot and Cori, Andrew and Lexa, Travis Lathrop, Mesa Ruiz, Cortney and Jake Seltman, Amy Sturtz, Muse Lokajikova, Joy Dyanne Stearns, Linda

Meacci, Cristin Cepull-Perney, Maureen Tighe, and Ellen Rubin. Thank you to Martín Prechtel, whose teachings offered orienting landmarks which helped us navigate the labyrinthine territory of our grief. And to our extended community, who sang, who grew corn, who wept, and those who said, "I have no words."

To Jizo, Bodhisattva, also called Earth Store, who, in Zen Buddhism, never abandons the souls of travelers and children and who accompanied us on this grief journey ... and wears a little red bib.

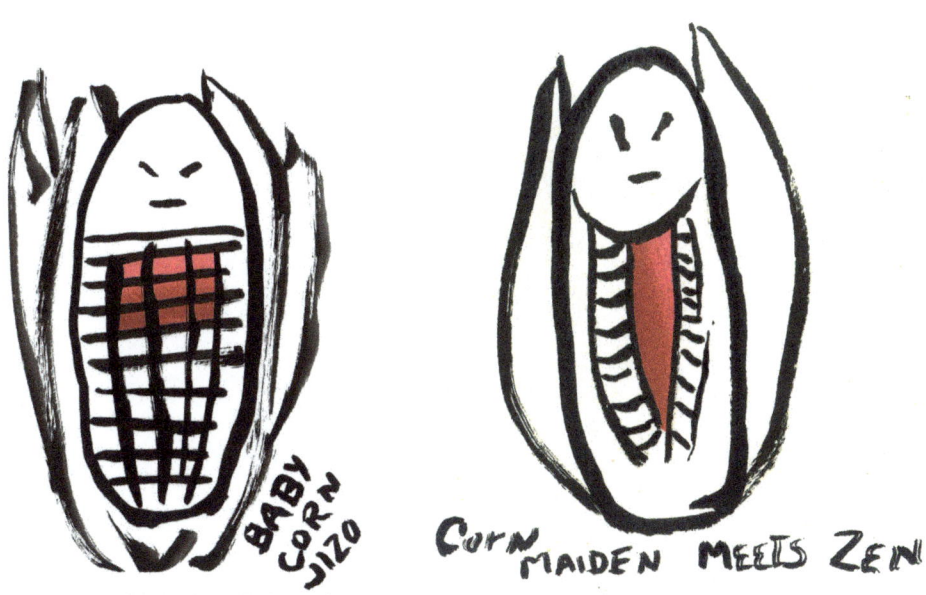

BABY CORN JIZO

CORN MAIDEN MEETS ZEN

LIST OF ART WORKS

SOURCES QUOTED

Mirabal, Robert, and Zink, Nelson. (2011). *Believe in the Corn: Manual for Puebloan Corn Growing.* Blurb Books.

Logghe, Hope. (2011, February). "Birthing Back our Roots: Yiya Vi Kagingdi Española Community Doulas." *Green Fire Times, Vol. 3, No. 2. News & Views from the Sustainable Southwest.* Publisher, Skip Whitson Green Fire Publishing LLC. Retrieved from http://www.greenfiretimes.com

JOAN LOGGHE

Joan Logghe has lived a life of poetry in La Puebla, New Mexico, where she and her husband, Michael, built their solar houses, raised three children, have five grandkids, and one great grandson. She has taught extensively, all ages, from UNM-Los Alamos to children in central Europe. She has led a yearly workshop at Ghost Ranch since 1990, taught at Santa Clara Pueblo day school, and, for 21 years, at the Santa Fe Girls' School. Over and over, she has experienced the salutary power of poetry. She has run art and writing workshops, AIDS writing circles, and workshops for crisis, illness, and loss. Joan was Santa Fe's Poet Laureate from 2010–2012. She has inspired and edited countless books by children and adults and served as Poetry Editor for Peggy O'Mara's *Mothering Magazine* for many years. Her awards include a National Endowment for the Arts Fellowship, Witter Bynner Foundation for Poetry Grants, a Mabel Dodge Luhan Internship, and a Barbara Deming/Money for Women grant. Her books include *What Makes a Woman Beautiful* (Pennywhistle Press), *Twenty Years in Bed with the Same Man* (La Alameda Press), *Sophia* (La Alameda Press), *Another Desert: Jewish Poetry of New Mexico* (edited with Miriam Sagan, Sherman Asher Press), *Blessed Resistance* (Mariposa Printing & Publishing), *Rice* (Tres Chicas Books), *Love & Death: Greatest Hits* (with Miriam Sagan and Renée Gregorio, Tres Chicas Books), *The Singing Bowl* (UNM Press), and *Unpunctuated Awe: Poems of Santa Fe* (Tres Chicas Books).

Corina Sophia Logghe

Corina Logghe, Joan's daughter, Hope's big sister, *Tia* Corina, co-manages the Española Farmer's Market and spends the rest of her days making beauty in the form of sewing, eco-printing, and garden tending. She also is an events manager, dance instructor, and mother to her son, Galen. She is a magical auntie who regularly invites her nieces down to her porch for creative time.

Hope Logghe

Hope Logghe is a Lactation Consultant providing care to rural communities in Northern New Mexico. Hope worked at a milk bank in Pittsburgh and supported bereaved families in donating their precious milk to medically vulnerable infants. She trains medical providers to give care to newly bereaved families. As a lactation consultant with a local home visiting program, she provides in-home lactation support to families. She lives with her husband, Leland, and their two beautiful daughters, Kaleia and Krystal, who fill the land with trampoline laughter. Krystal says, "I wish I got to see Jade. Why I didn't was because I was born two years after. Having a sister I didn't meet is kinda sad." Their home is located in rural Northern New Mexico, on the land of Hope's birth, between her parents and her sister, and beside the garden where Jade Bird was planted like a seed. Contact her at www.jadeheartcare.com.

Leland Guthrie

Leland is a depth psychologist in private practice in Northern New Mexico. He spends his free time practicing ancestral skills, painting, and tending to the human and more-than-human beings in his small corner of the Universe, including his wife and two kids, gardens, pets, and a flock of chickens.

Kaleia Amaya Guthrie

Kaleia was just turning three when she lost her sister. Included here are three poems she dictated to her mother soon after Jade's passing. She is a student at Acequia Madre Elementary. She makes art, plays violin, sings in chorus, and does creative dance. Her painting *Corn Sisters* on the front cover was created at age 11.

Kaleia dictated this to Hope:

The Moonshine

The moon is rising from the mountaintops
The moon is falling down from the trees
The earth is tumbling down and up
And the butterflies are flying up
The birds are singing from the mountaintops
Around your ears
Your ears are falling from your cheeks
Your sunrise is falling up
And winter sun
And how you great and nearly shore
Corn rolls down the path
Sprinkle them and the path is sun
1, 2, 3, 4
Passageway! Passageway!
...and sprinkle the corn seed all along.

Out the west window

white banty rooster

red-winged blackbirds

our baby's grave

I am a wealthy woman

The body text of *Jade Bird: Singing Grief* is set in Baskerville, a serif typeface designed in the 1750s by John Baskerville, a groundbreaking artist who began as a calligrapher and carver of gravestones. A tombstone Baskerville cut in 1730 shows the first instance of this font's crisp, generous proportions, the cornerstone of his impassioned ambition to create books of the highest quality, showcasing his innovations in press technology, ink, and paper. In the preface to Milton's Paradise Lost, Baskerville wrote of his desire to print "...such only as are books of Consequence..." making the designer's choice of this font a consummate fit for poet Logghe's exquisite—consequential—book.

The titles herein are set in the delicate serif typeface Perpetua, designed by sculptor and stonemason Eric Gill, commissioned to echo both the unique lettering he carved into his war memorials and tombstones and his own elegant handwriting. Gill was asked to design a unique typeface, script as inscription, a serene face meant to calm, comfort, and be read by many. Perpetua is named for the Christian martyr Vibia Perpetua, an ardent diarist whose writings recount her grief, her faith, and her dreams and visions; she is the Patron Saint of mothers and expectant mothers. Both typefaces serve as grace notes to this book, a collaborative act of deep Beauty-Making and itself, Grace.